HONEY

Uses & Medicinal Properties of the Oldest Sweetner of the World with Home Remedies

Dr. Rajeev Sharma

MANOJ PUBLICATIONS

Publishers
Manoj Publications
761, Main Road, Burari, Delhi-110084
Ph: 27611116, 27611349, Fax : 27611546
Mobile : 9868112194
E-mail : *info@manojpublications.com*
Website : *www.manojpublications.com*

Showroom :
Manoj Publications
1583-84, Dariba Kalan, Chandni Chowk, Delhi-6
Ph. : 23262174, 23268216 (Mob) 9818753569

ISBN : 978-81-310-0743-3

First Edition : 2009

HONEY : Dr. Rajeev Sharma

PREFACE

Honey is a treat, and is man's oldest sweetener. It is an excellent substitute for sugar in our drinks and food. It is also good for many medicinal uses and treating certain conditions.

Honey is composed of sugars like glucose and fructose and minerals like magnesium, potassium, calcium, sodium chlorine, sulphur, iron and phosphate.

It contains many vitamins all of which change according to the qualities of the nectar and pollen. Several kinds of hormones are also present in it. Approximately one half of the human diet is derived directly or indirectly from crops pollinated by bees. Today honeybees are an essential part of a healthy agriculture economy.

If you have allergies, honey can be beneficial. If you eat honey that is local to your area, it may help prevent your seasonal allergies. Bees use the pollen from local plants and eventually it ends up in your honey.

Honey may also be good for your skin. It has the ability to attract water. It is also safe for sensitive skin. You can use it as a moisturizing mask for your skin as well as your hair.

In this book the subject is covered to its full. We try our best to cover every aspect of honey, its medicinal and industrial use along with home remedies.

—Publishers

CONTENTS

MIRACULOUS HONEY

Honey is a treat, and is man's oldest sweetener. It is an excellent substitute for sugar in our drinks and food. It is also good for many medicinal uses and treating certain conditions. Reliance on commercialized medicines which contain too many chemicals can become hazardous to our health.

Honey is composed of sugars like glucose and fructose and minerals like magnesium, potassium, calcium, sodium chlorine, sulphur, iron and phosphate.

It contains vitamins B_1, B_2, C, B_6, B_5 and B_3 all of which change according to the qualities of the nectar and pollen. Besides the above, copper, iodine, and zinc exist in it in small quantities. Several kinds of hormones are also present in it. Approximately one half of the human diet is derived directly or indirectly from crops pollinated by bees. Today honeybees are an essential part of a healthy agriculture economy.

If you have allergies, honey can be beneficial. If you eat honey that is local to your area, it may help prevent your seasonal allergies. Bees use the pollen from local plants and eventually it ends up in your honey.

Honey may also be good for your skin. It has the ability to attract water. It is also safe for sensitive skin. You can use it as a moisturizing mask for your skin as well as your hair. To use it as a conditioner, mix the honey with olive oil. Be sure to wash your hair thoroughly before you go outside.

If you have a sore throat, take some honey. Honey has

powerful antimicrobial properties, which can soothe your raw tissues. Pour a teaspoon of honey into a large serving spoon and then top off the spoon with lemon juice. Swallow the concoction (without water) every few hours until symptoms clear up. Some people add a pinch of black pepper to increase blood circulation to the throat. Due to its natural anti-inflammatory effect, it will help to heal the wounds more quickly. It also has different phytochemicals—chemicals found in plants and different foods—that kill viruses, bacteria, and fungus making it a good substitute for wound dressings. The taste may also take your mind off the pain. There is evidence that honey diluted in water will help with your stomach aches and dehydration.

Do you have a cut? Honey is a natural antiseptic. Medical journals cite more than 600 cases in which honey was employed to treat wounds. By applying honey to your wounds, you prevent infections. Honey contains antimicrobial agents, which prevents infections by killing the bacteria in and around your wounds. When using honey it may help to heat it little before putting it on your wound. Many types of bacteria can't survive in honey, so wounds heal, swelling eases, and tissue can grow back.

Honey may also be effective in the treatment of your ulcers.In Europe, honey has been used internally to help cure ulcers, particularly stomach ulcers. Burns, too, heal better with honey. The advantage of honey is that it not only prevents infections from occurring, it actually accelerates skin healing. Since the sugar in honey absorbs water it helps to trap some of the moisture so that the bacteria and other microbes can't grow as easily as in other food.

In treating diarrhoea, honey promotes the rehydration of the body and more quickly clears up the diarrhoea and any vomiting and stomach upsets. The anti-bacterial properties of honey, both the peroxide and non-peroxide, are effective in the laboratory against MRSA strains of bacteria which are notoriously resistant to antibiotics and are sometimes responsible for the closing of hospital wards.

For centuries honey has been regarded as a wonderful gift of nature in which the properties of an excellent food, beneficial alike to adults and children, are combined with medicinal properties. Ancient Russian manuscripts attached great importance to honey as a medicine. Popular medicine has successfully used it for many diseases from time immemorial. The results of experiments and observations made by the medical science in recent decades have proved that honey is an important medicine possessing many-sided therapeutic properties.

Honey is very effective in the treatment of some pathological conditions of the intestinal tract, the respiratory organs, the heart, and the nerves.

HOENY IN ANCIENT LITERATURE

The description about honey is found in the literature of almost every country of the world. It means it is and was famous world wide.

21st Century B.C.

Honey is alluded to in the Sumerian and Babylonian cuneiform writings, The Hittite Code, the sacred writings of India, the Vedas and in the ancient writings of Egypt.

Biblical

The area now comprising Israel and the Palestine autonomous region is often referred to as 'the land of milk and honey.'

Ancient Egypt : 40th Century B.C.

Honey was used in most households as a sweetening agent. The people of this time valued honey highly, thus, it was commonly used as a tribute or payment. Honey was also used to feed sacred animals.

Sumeria, Assyria and Babylonia 21st Century B.C.

Honey was poured over thresholds and stones bearing commemorative offerings. Honey and wine were also poured over bolts that were to be used in sacred buildings.

Greece

An ancient custom was the offering of honey to the gods and to spirits of the dead. Mead, an alcohol drink made with honey, was considered the drink of the gods.

Germany: 11th Century A.D.

German beer was sweetened with honey. German peasants were required to give their feudal lords a payment of honey and beeswax.

America

Conquering Spaniards found that the natives of 16th century A D. Mexico and Central America had already developed beekeeping. A distinct family of honey bees were native to the America.

American Colonies: 17th Century A.D.

European settlers introduced European honey bees to New England in about 1638. North American natives called these honey bees the 'white man's flies.'

Honey was used to prepare food and beverages, to make cement, to preserve fruits, to concoct furniture paste-polish and varnish and for medicinal purposes.

An Ancient Medicine Rediscovered

Honey is one of the oldest medicines. Its use is recorded in Sumerian clay tablets estimated to be 4,000 years old, and in Egyptian papyri dated from 1900 to 1250 B.C. It is also mentioned in the Vedas, the sacred scriptures of Hinduism, thought to be about 5,000 years old, and in the Holy Qu'ran and the Talmud. Hippocrates (460-357 B.C.) used many of the Egyptian prescriptions. He found that honey 'cleans sores and ulcers of the lips, heals carbuncles and running sores.'

Celsus used honey for many different purposes: as a laxative, as a cure for diarrhoea and upset stomach, for coughs and throat maladies, to agglutinate wounds and for eye diseases. Honey has continued to be used in medicine ever since, but little was known about how it worked. It was not until the late 19th century that bacteria were found to be the cause of infections. Although there are several reports in medical journals in the 1930's of honey being effective in clearing wounds of bacterial infection, it was not recognized in these reports that it had been established in laboratory work in 1919 that honey has antibacterial activity.

It was not until the mid-1940's that more intensive laboratory studies were carried out, but by this time antibiotics were becoming available for the treatment of infections, and honey was displaced from use in medicine. Despite the advent of antibiotics, honey has continued to be used in folk medicine, and it is from this pool of knowledge that the re-introduction of honey into modern medicine has come. There have been numerous reports in medical journals of this folk remedy being used as a last resort on infected wounds, burns and ulcers that were not responding to antibiotic treatment. The remedy was in all cases found to be remarkably effective. This effectiveness is being recognized in an increasing number of reports. In 1989, an editorial in the Journal of the Royal Society of Medicine expressed the opinion that "the time has now come for conventional medicine to lift the blinds off this 'traditional remedy' and to give it its due recognition."

THE DELICIOUS FORMS OF HONEY

Most of us know honey as a sweet, golden liquid. But, in fact, honey can be found in a variety of forms.

Comb Honey : Comb honey is honey that comes as it was produced—in the honey bees' wax comb. The comb, as well as the honey, is edible!

Cut Comb : Cut comb honey is liquid honey that has added chunks of the honey comb in the jar. Also known as liquid-cut comb combination.

Liquid Honey : Free of visible crystals, liquid honey is extracted from the honey comb by centrifugal force, gravity or straining. Because liquid honey mixes easily into a variety of foods, it's especially convenient for cooking and baking. Most of the honey produced is sold in the liquid form.

Naturally Crystallized Honey : Naturally crystallized honey is honey that part of the natural glucose content has spontaneously crystallized from solution as the monohydrate.

Whipped (or Creamed) Honey : While all honey will crystallize in time, whipped honey (also known as creamed honey or sugared honey) is brought to market in a crystallized state. The crystallization is controlled so that, at room temperature, the honey can be spread like butter. In many countries around the world, whipped honey is preferred to the liquid form.

Honey Products : Honey products do not meet the compositional criteria for honey, but are products consisting in whole or in part of honey.

Dried Honey : Dried honey is honey that has been dehydrated and mixed with other ingredients to keep it free-flowing.

Flavoured/Fruited Honey : Flavored/Fruited honey is honey that has either fruit, colouring or flavouring added.

Honey Stix : Honey stix consist of liquid honey in a straw. Sometimes flavours are added.

Infused Honey : Infused honey is honey that has had flavours of herbs, spices, peels, etc. added to it by steeping.

VARITIES OF HONEY

It will be too strange for any honey fan to not know at least some different honey varieties and understand their characteristics so as to be able to cleverly use and apply them in different foods.

Acacia

Acacia is made from nectar collected from Acacia tree blossoms which produce a honey that is remarkably clear and pure. It is one of the most popular and sweetest honey varieties because of its mild delicate floral taste. It can remain in a liquid state for a long period of time due to its high concentration of fructose. Because of its low sucrose content, it is the best choice for diabetics. Known for its

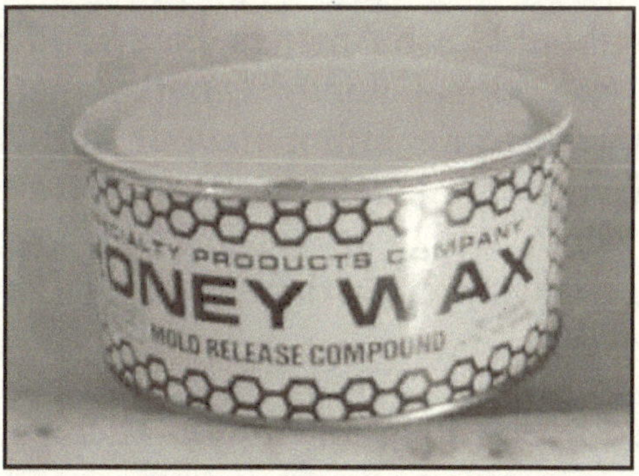

therapeutic action, Acacia cleanses the liver, regulates the intestinc, and is anti-inflammatory for the respiratory system. This honey is excellent for sweetening without altering the taste or the aroma of beverages. It's so mild that it doesn't affect the tea's aroma which you would want to retain. Also, kids love this honey. Its sweetness also perfectly balances the salty tang of the cheese.

Alfalfa

Alfalfa honey, produced extensively throughout Canada and the United States from the purple or blue blossoms, is light in colour with a subtle spicy profile and mildly scented floral aroma. Its delicate nature doesn't overpower other flavours making it a favourite choice for chefs for their baked foods and a fine table honey for tea lovers. Not as sweet as most honey, it is a preferred choice for combining with other ingredients or straight from the jar.

Avocado

Its name is a misnomer. Avocado honey tastes nothing like the fruit, avocado. Collected from the California avocado blossoms, avocado honey is dark in colour and has a fairly rich and buttery flavour. This honey originated in Southern Mexico and is now a common crop in Central America, Australia and other tropical regions.

Basswood

Produced from the cream-coloured Basswood blossoms found throughout North America, Basswood honey is one of the few exceptional honey varieties that has a light colour and yet strong biting flavour and a distinctive lingering flavour. It's somewhat fresh, pleasant 'woody' scent is very good with teas like Earl Grey and works well for salad dressings and marinades.

Blueberry

Produced in New England and in Michigan, Blueberry honey is taken from the tiny white flowers of the blueberry bush. It is typically light amber in colour, has a pleasant flavour, a slight tang, and a blueberry aftertaste. A good table honey.

Buckwheat

Now unusual and hard to find, Buckwheat honey is produced in Minnesota, New York, Ohio, Pennsylvania and Wisconsin as well as in eastern Canada. It is dark, full-bodied, and rich in iron—a key reason which it's popular with honey lovers. Buckwheat honey has been found to contain more antioxidant compounds than some lighter honeys. It is perhaps the strongest and darkest of honey varieties. Most experts recommend using a strong-tasting type of honey, such as buckwheat for mead production, since the honey is diluted.

Clover

Originating from Canada and New Zealand, Clover honey is one of the most widely available and popular honey varieties. White clover in particular is grown as a widespread blooming pasture crop and is a major nectar source in many parts of the world. This classic honey has such a pleasingly mild sweet that anyone find very easy to accept and perfect for use in light sauces, dressings and baking. Depending on the location and source, clover honey varies in colour from water white to light amber to amber.

Eucalyptus

Eucalyptus honey comes from one of the larger plant genera, containing over 500 distinct species and many hybrids. Its country of origin is Australia but produced largely in California. Widely available, it varies greatly in colour and flavour but tends to have a special herbal flavour which carries a hint of menthol. This honey is traditionally by many people as a protection against colds and headaches.

Fireweed

One of the most popular honeys, Fireweed comes from a tall perennial herb grown in the open woods of North West US. Light in colour, it has its own way of being sweet and complex at the same time. It has an extraordinary smooth, delicate, and buttery taste which is great for gourmet cooking, baking, glazing, grilling, meat and fish smoking.

Heather

Thick, amber in colour, Heather honey has one of the strongest and most pungent flavours. It is fragrant and floral with a very lingering aftertaste that is almost bitter. It is commonly served with ham, chicken, lamb, seafood and cold dishes and goes well with strong, black coffee. Prized since ancient times due to its medicinal properties, Heather honey is extremely high in protein content.

Leatherwood

Leatherwood honey comes from the leatherwood blossom—a native eucalypt found in the south-west of Tasmania, Australia and is the source for 70% of the country's honey. Established worldwide as a distinct honey type and a fine gourmet product, Leatherwood honey has a unique taste and strong floral flavour. Its distinctive spicy flavour makes it an excellent spread on wheat toast, and an ideal ingredient in recipes as it not only sweetens but adds a fantastic aroma to cakes, muffins, coffee and tea.

Linden

The small-leaved Linden tree which grows in moist, clay soil and has clusters of small, yellow-white fragrant flowers hanging from slender stems, is common throughout Denmark. It's planted in gardens, parks and along road sides, city streets and boulevards. Linden honey is one of those honey varieties that will completely change the misconception of those who think that honey is no more than just sugared water. It has a light yellow colour and a very distinctive yet delicate fresh woody scent. Because of its sedative and antiseptic qualities it is recommended in cases of anxiety and insomnia, whereby honey can be combined with a bath of linden blossoms before sleep. Linden honey is also used in the treatment of colds, cough and bronchitis.

Manuka

Found only in New Zealand's costal areas, Manuka

honey is collected from the flower of the Tea Tree bush. The Unique Manuka Factor found in some Manuka honey is an antibacterial property which is especially effective for healing of sore throats, colds, indigestion, stomach ulcer, acne and pimples. Some people find Manuka honey too 'medicinal' in taste but it goes well with tea or toast with or without butter!

Orange Blossom

Orange blossom honey, often a combination of citrus sources, is usually light in colour and mild in flavour with a fresh fruity scent, and a fragrant citrus taste. Orange blossom honey originated from Spain/Mexico but is produced in many countries.

Pumpkin Blossom

From the natural nectars of the Pumpkin Blossoms and harvested once a year in the early fall, Pumpkin Blossom honey is a dark amber-coloured liquid with a light floral fragrance. As a specialty gourmet varietal, it is an incredibly suitable topping for dishes and desserts and works well when paired with savory or spicy ingredients, like a barbeque sauce. When drizzled on sweet potatoes, yogurt and desserts, it also tastes great. Contrary to what its name suggests, Pumpkin honey does not taste like Pumpkin Pie at all. This honey is seasonal and limited as the bloom is short and does not produce much nectar.

Red Gum

Red Gum is a common Eucalypt found in Australia that produces one of the darker premium varieties of honey. Having a relatively higher level of antioxidants compared to the rest, red gum honey has a thick constituency, a bold taste (like buckwheat honey) and a distinctive aroma. It's also a favourite ingredient in bread baking and meat marinades.

Rewarewa

Full bodied and malty, Rewarewa honey comes from

a bright red needle-like flowers grown in the bushy hills and valleys of New Zealand. This classic dark red premium honey possesses a caramel-like and slightly burnt flavour that makes it popular natural sweetener for hot drinks and a spread. It is ideal for both sweet and savoury dishes and is well-known for use in oriental dishes.

Pine Tree

Pine Tree honey (sometimes also known as forest honey, fir honey, honeydew or tea tree honey) consists of the majority of the total honey production. It is not particularly sweet, tastes a little bitter, has a strong aroma, and is relatively rich in minerals and proteins. It is rather resistant to crystallization.

Sourwood

Contrary to its name, Sourwood honey is not sour, but sweet like any honey. This light-coloured, delicate, subtle honey has an almost caramel or buttery flavour, and a pleasant, lingering aftertaste. With this honey, you don't need any more butter on your biscuits or bread!

Sage

Sage honey, primarily produced in California, is light in colour, heavy bodied and has a mild but delightful flavour. It is extremely slow to granulate, making it a favourite honey variety among honey packers for blending with other honeys to slow down granulation.

Tawari

Originating from the creamy white flowers of New Zealand's Tawari trees, this honey has a golden colour and a creamy butterscotch flavour. So subtle and mild, it's a perfect chef choice for topping desserts such as pancakes, waffles or ice-cream.

Tupelo

Clear yellow in colour, with a characteristic greenish glow, Tupelo honey is a premium honey produced in northwest Florida. It is heavy bodied and is usually light golden amber with a greenish cast and has a mild, distinctive taste. Because of the high fructose content, Tupelo honey is one of the sweetest honey varieties and it hardly granulates.

Wildflower

Also known as 'multifloral' or 'mixed floral' honey, Wildflower is often used to describe honey varieties from miscellaneous and undefined flower sources. Its colour can vary from very light to dark and flavour range from light and fruity to tangy and rich, depending on the mix from the different seasonal wildflowers.

Blended

Most commercially available honey is blended. It is a mixture of two or more honeys differing in floral source, colour, flavour, density or geographic origin.

Polyfloral

Polyfloral honey is derived from the nectar of many types of flowers.

Monofloral

Different monofloral honeys have a distinctive flavour and colour due to differences between their principal nectar sources. Beekeepers keep monofloral beehives in an area where the bees have access to only one type of flower, because of that flower's properties. In practice, because of the difficulties in containing bees, a small proportion of any honey will be from additional nectar from other flower types.

GOOD QUALITY HONEY

Even after deciding that a certain floral variety of honey would be your most favourite type of honey, many of us are often still left with the question of "How do I choose the same floral variety of honey amongst all the countless brands of honey from all over the world, with a big range of prices in the market place?" When I am navigating through the maze of all the different honey in the shops, I look out for certain specific information to ensure that the honey I buy is value for money. Good quality honey, that is, honey of value can be judged by five key factors, namely:

Water content : Good quality honey essentially has low water content. Honey is likely to ferment and lose its freshness if the water content of honey is greater than 19%. The reason is that all unpasteurized honey contains wild yeasts. Due to the high sugar concentration, these yeasts will pose little risk in low moisture honey because osmosis will draw sufficient water from the yeast to force them into dormancy. In honey that has a higher proportion of water, the yeast may survive and cause fermentation to begin in storage. This results an increase of acidity, which then becomes an important quality criteria.

Honey is very hygroscopic, which means that it easily absorbs moisture from the air. Thus, in areas with a very high humidity it can be difficult to produce good quality honey of sufficiently low water content, which can be measured using a gadget called refractometer. Raw honey's moisture content can be as low as 14%, and is usually deemed as more valuable and hence is relatively more costly. Honey containing up to 20% water is not recommended for mead-making. One simple way of judging the relative quantity of water in honey involves taking two same-size, same-temperature, well-sealed jars of honey from different sources. Turn the two jars upside-down and watch the bubbles rise. Bubbles in the honey with more water content will rise faster.

HMF (Hydroxymethylfurfural) : HMF is a break-down product of fructose (one of the main sugars in honey) formed slowly during storage and very quickly when honey is heated. The amount of HMF present in honey is therefore used as a guide to storage guide to storage length and the amount of heating which has taken place. HMF's occurrence and accumulation in honey is variable depending on honey type. High levels of HMF may indicate excessive heating during the extraction process. Honey that is traded in a bulk form is usually required to be below 10 or 15mg/kg to enable further processing and then give some shelf life before a level of 40 mg/kg is reached. It is not uncommon for honey sold in hot climates to be well over 100 mg/kg in HMF. This is mostly due to the ambient temperatures (over 35°C) that honey is exposed to in the distribution channel. Some countries set an HMF limit for imported honey. You may also want to note the colour of the honey as it can sometimes be an indicator of quality because honey becomes darker during storage and heating.

Inverted Sugars : High levels of HMF (greater than 100 mg/kg) can also be an indicator of adulteration with inverted sugars. Cane sugar or sucrose, is 'inverted' by heating with a food acid, and this process creates HMF. Many food items sweetened with high fructose corn syrups, *e.g.* carbonated soft drinks, can have levels of HMF up to 1,000 mg/kg.

Colour : Honey is colour graded into light, amber, and dark categories which do not really have any bearing on quality. Some of the most distinctively and strongly flavoured honey varieties, such as basswood, are very light, while very mild and pleasant honeys such as tulip poplar can be quite dark. Honey colour is measured on the scale in millimeters. While it is not an indicator of honey quality and there are exceptions to the rule, generally speaking, the darker colour the honey, the higher its mineral contents, the pH readings, and the aroma/flavour levels. Minerals such as potassium, chlorine, sulfur, iron, manganese, magnesium, and sodium have been found to be much higher in darker honeys.

TESTING PURE HONEY

How can you differentiate 100% pure honey and adulterated honey?

The term 'adulterated honey' implies that the honey has been added glucose, dextrose, molasses, corn syrup, sugar syrup, invert sugar, flour, starch, or any other similar product, other than the floral nectar gathered, processed, and stored in the comb by honey bees. Legal standards and requirements for foods, including honey quality, and tests for honey adulteration vary widely amongst countries and some may not meet the wish of every consumer around the world.

Personally, when selecting honey in the shop, I think it's almost impossible to tell the bad from the good by just looking at the honey content through the bottle or studying

its food and nutrition labels. My take is always—go for the trusted or more known brands. We all know that a 'pure honey' label doesn't guarantee at all that it is not diluted with water and further sweetened with corn syrup; it just promises that there is real pure honey inside, with no suggestion of its amount. The law does not require a 'pure honey' label to say how much pure honey is in the bottle. Some honey brands you get from the markets don't carry any ingredients list and this is enough to make feel suspicious of the quality. Also, prices are not always a good indication of quality honey. In food fraud cases, manufacturers can mix different honey floral blends and sell it as more expensive varieties such as Manuka honey. And so-called 'local honey' may not be locally produced and processed local honey but cheap, low quality honey imported from other countries but bottled and distributed locally.

A common misconception is that granulated or crystallized honey is proof of adulteration with sugar water. The truth is honey is a supersaturated sugar solution and can granulate whether or not it has been adulterated, so crystallization is normal, especially in temperate climates. Furthermore, some honey from certain floral sources is especially prone to crystallization. Buying honey in the comb is one way to assure ourselves of a quality product. Comb honey is sealed in the hive by the bees; therefore consumers can be confident that the honey has not been adulterated with sugar water. However, to boost honey production, some irresponsible beekeepers feed their bees with sugar syrup so that the bees can convert the syrup to 'honey'. What these bees produced is honey that is adulterated, very clear and runny, just like syrup.

Some people say that ants don't fancy pure honey and will not hover around it. The reason why a sweet liquid is more attractive than another for the ants could be due to the liquid density and we know that honey viscosity varies depending on its floral type.

Another test that is commonly discussed is the flame test which involves lighting up a cotton bud dipped into the honey with a match-stick flame. It's believed that the honey will burn if it's pure. I have tried this method many times using different types of honey, some of which I was very sure they're pure honey (*e.g* honeycomb honey), but the result I got was never consistent, and it seemed to depend very much on how much honey was dipped and how long the honey was exposed to the flame.

There's another simple way which I have tried to verify the purity of honey: Observe how liquid honey comes down into a glass of water. Pure honey does not immediately dissolve in water; you will notice that it takes a bit of effort to stir it in the water to dissolve the lumpy bits, whereas sugar tends to dissolve easily in a jiggery as you drop them into the water. However, test result is sometimes not that clear because different honey varieties have different viscosity, some are denser and thicker than others, and obviously honey in cream form, even if it's adulterated with other substance, will not dissolve as easy as liquid honey in water.

It is suggested that people who are used to tasting honey may be easier to detect any added sugar. But frankly, because there are just too many floral varieties and blends, and the amount of adulteration may not be sufficient to affect the taste and aroma of the honey, even though I frequently take honey, I am still not 100% certain about my suspicion sometimes.

Hence, it's hard to be really absolutely sure about honey authenticity, unless from home you can perform scientific laboratory test like spectroscopy, a method that uses the principle of interaction of light with mater to differentiate substances or conduct carbon isotope ratios analysis to determine if sugars were added to the honey (don't bother if these jargons sound totally bizarre; as a consumer, I am not familiar with them either).

Nevertheless, from all the verification ways that are

discussed above (labels, pouring, dissolving honey, etc) if you have reasons to suspect that the honey is diluted and corn syrup has been added, my stance is - stay away from those brands. Better to err on the side of caution than to be sorry...well, you most probably won't fall sick by taking the adulterated honey, but you know adulteration with cheaper sugars brings down the natural value of the honey and this doesn't help in justifying for the amount of money you pay.

DISTINGUISHING QUALITY HONEY

The high quality natural honey can be distinguished by its fragrance and taste. The best period to stock up honey is in summer, when it is being collected in large quantities. The ripe, freshly collected, high quality honey at 20°C (68°F) flows from the knife in a straight squirt, without breaking into separate drops. After falling down the honey should form a clear hillock. A saying goes: "the honey rustles and glues like viscose." The ripe honey is being collected from the sealed honey combs, therefore it should always be of high quality.

The honey should not lay down in layers. If this is a case, it indicates the excessive humidity (over 20%) of the product, and such a honey would not be suitable for long term preservation.

A fluffy thin layer on the surface of the honey (like a white foam), or marble-coloured and white spots in crystallized honey at the wallsides of the bottle are caused by filling of liquid honey with subsequent sealing—the air bubbles are surfacing and part of them is concentrated at the wallsides. This is an indication of a high quality honey, which was filled without pasteurization (heating).

If the honey is transparent, burning with amber-like colours, then (unless it is very fresh) it has most likely been heated and is of little value. Transparent and reluctant to thicken honey can also indicate its being a result of feeding the bees with sugar syrup or even sugar itself, which is bad both for the bees and for the honey they produce, as naturally they are supposed to feed on flower nectar.

A true honey that is at least one month old is usually of demure (not translucent) colours.

Colour, Flavour and Form

Honeys differ in colour and flavour depending on what blossoms the honey bees visit in search of nectar. Honey colour ranges from almost colourless to dark amber brown and its flavour varies from delectably mild to richly bold. As a general rule, light-coloured honey is milder in taste and dark-coloured honey is stronger.

Honey comes in a variety of forms including liquid, whipped and comb. Free of any crystals or wax, liquid honey is extracted from the comb in the hive by centrifugal force, gravity, straining or other means. Whipped honey (also known as creamed honey) is finely crystallized so that it remains creamy and spreadable. Comb honey is honey that comes as it was produced in the honey bees' wax comb.

❑❑

HEALING POWER OF HONEY

You probably have it in your kitchen and eat it on toast a few mornings each week, but did you know that honey has the power to cure allergies and prevent cancer? It's true. Honey is one of natures most perfect foods. Raw honey is made from pollen and while large doses of pollen can irritate allergies; small doses, which are consumed on a regular basis, will eliminate them. That is why it is important to buy honey from a local producer. The daily pollen that you are receiving through the air, is the same pollen that you have formed an allergy to. Local honey is made from this same pollen. By eating honey everyday, you can build your own immunity to the allergy. This immune booster is natural and delicious!

Honey contains vitamins, minerals, and amino acids and is a wonderful beauty aid that nourishes the skin and the hair. Honey is often referred to as 'Mother Nature's Fountain of Youth' as it has properties that can reduce and sometimes retard wrinkles and fine lines from appearing. Honey acts as an antibacterial and anti fungal agent and helps disinfect and speed the healing process in wounds, scrapes and burns. Some ancient languages also refer to the importance of honey.

China is currently by far the largest honey producing nation in the world, with around 40 per cent of the market. The next largest producers are the US, Argentina and Ukraine. Also starting to emerge onto the world honey production arena are Thailand and Vietnam. Remember, honey is best when purchased raw, pasteurization can kill most of the healing properties of honey. This is another reason that buying locally is you in your best interest.

There have been many research studies on the health benefits of honey. In one study, 25 people were told to eat between four and 10 tablespoons of buckwheat honey, depending on their weight, each day for a month. They could eat the honey in almost any form, but it couldn't be baked or dissolved in tea. Many chose to eat straight from the spoon. Antioxidant levels rose in the participants. Antioxidants provide defence against free radicals, which cause cell damage. Researchers discovered honey contained as many antioxidants—which combat the free radicals which can damage cells—as spinach, apples, oranges or strawberries.

Scientists from the University of Illinois say honey appears to have a 'mild protective effect'. Health-promoting compounds found in honey could make this ingredient a more attractive option for food makers currently using bulk sweeteners such as high-fructose corn syrup and looking to jump on board the growing health foods trend. Honey may be a healthier alternative to corn syrup due to its higher level of antioxidants, compounds which are believed to fight cancer, heart disease and other diseases.

Honey, which contains a number of antioxidant components that act as preservatives, also shows promise as a replacement for some synthetic antioxidants widely used as preservatives in many of the foods found in our grocery stores today.

A well known recipe for sore throat relief:

Honey Soother *(Makes 4 servings)*

Ingredients:

3 tea bags green or black

1 cinnamon stick

3 cups boiling water

1/4 cup honey

1 cup grapefruit juice

Directions : Place tea bags and cinnamon stick in a 1-quart tea pot. Add boiling water; steep 3 to 5 minutes. Remove cinnamon stick and tea bags; discard. Stir in grapefruit juice and honey.

❑❑

AMAZING BENEFITS OF HONEY

Honey is better than what most people think...

Not only does this delectable stimulate your taste buds and whet your appetite, its unique taste and aroma has sprung off many time honour cooking ideas and recipes such as the cannot-be-missed honey baked toasts and honey dips. But is honey really good for you? This caramel-like liquid seems to be full of calories. ...sure it tastes good and has a pleasant texture that coats the irritated throat, but perhaps it's just a little more than a tasty placebo...

The fact is, more and more researchers are turning up new evidence of honey's medical benefits in all directions. The benefits of honey don't just stop at satisfying the palate; honey also offers incredible antiseptic, antioxidant and cleansing properties for our body and health, hot beauty and skin care tips for ladies, and amazing healing properties as a head-to-toe remedy, from eye conjunctivitis to athlete foot.

Its powerful healing attributes have long been used thousands of years ago and known to promote healing for cuts, cure ailments and diseases, and correct health disorders for generations after generations. The renowned UMF Manuka honey, perhaps the tastiest natural medicine, is commonly cited in many discussions on health benefits of honey. It not only fights infection and aids tissue healing but also helps reduce inflammation and scarring. In addition, it is often used for treating digestive problems such as diarrhoea, indigestion, stomach ulcers and gastroenteritis. With more and more health experts and theories supporting its benefits, this oldest natural sweetener just keeps getting better.

One of the greatest pleasure and fascination in using honey is understanding the different floral varieties of honey, their appearance and quality, and experimenting with each of their unique taste and distinct flavour, and being able to know which floral variety of honey is most perfect for which kind of foods. The uses and benefits of honey in foods are as diverse as its floral varieties and places of origin.

Facts about Honey

It is believed that honey history dated as far back as 10 to 20 million years ago and the practice of beekeeping to produce honey, apiculture, dates back to at least 700 BC.

In ancient times, Eygptians sacrificed honey by the tons to their river gods, Roman legions slathered honey on

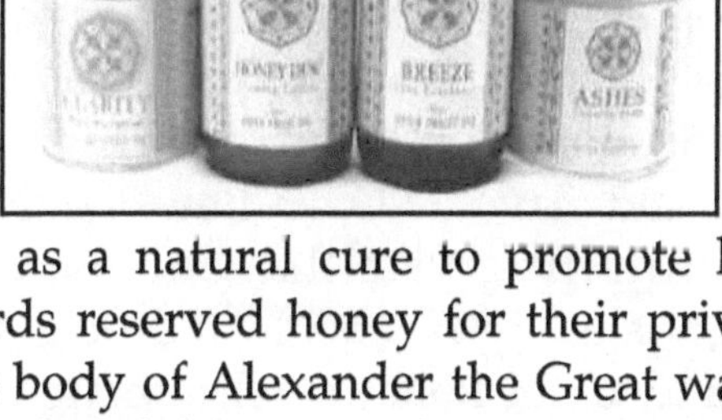

the wounds as a natural cure to promote healing, and medieval lords reserved honey for their private use. It's told that the body of Alexander the Great was preserved and embalmed with honey. As honey was then expensive and not all could afford it, its use in cooking was reserved only for the wealthy. And ancient myths and writings on alcoholic beverages throughout the world also contain references to mead, or honey wine, which is known as the world's oldest fermented berverage.

The biblical history also contains honey facts related to its benefits and goodness. Honey, a delicacy fit for the kings and queens!

When refined sugar made from sugar cane came along, it provided a relatively inexpensive alternative form of sweetening and began to displace honey for culinary use. The benefits of honey since then became more focused on its medicinal properties and its use in fine gourmet and confectionary.

Today, the word 'honey' has gone beyond its association with its benefits as a food and has crept deep into many cultures and languages.

Expiration of Honey

All nectar contains some kind of yeast which can reproduce in higher-moisture content honey and cause fermentation. While fermentation does not necessarily pose any health risk, some manufacturers do pasteurization whereby the honey is heated very quickly to kill any yeast cell without damaging the product too much and then rapidly cooled. Pasteurized honey also has a slower granulation process and will last longer in its liquid state.

While one of the greatest facts on honey storage is that it doesn't spoil even with no preservatives and additives, liquid honey is susceptible to physical and chemical changes during storage; it tends to darken and lose some of its aroma and flavour. Over time, liquid honey also tends to naturally crystallise and become lumpy. Crystallisation is easily reversible and does not affect the taste and quality of the honey at all, although it changes its appearance. Hence, for commercial reasons, a certain shelf life is often stated on the honey bottles in the shop.

HONEY AS A MEDICINE

In all of ancient history, honey has been a constant part of medicine. Honey has very high levels of antioxidants, comparable to the levels in spinach, apples and strawberries. Antioxidants are very important to our health because they rid our system of damaging free radicals that cause cell damage. There are so many more uses for honey other than in your tea or cereal. Below are just some of the most commonly used medicinal remedies that are made from honey.

❑ Honey has great antibacterial factors. It is not known exactly why honey is antibacterial, but studies have proven over and over again that honey is a great substance to use on wounds. Since honey is such a thick fluid, it breaks down the bacteria over time and does not allow it to grow again. Honey has been proven to be more effective in preventing infection in wounds than hydrogen peroxide.

❑ Honey can also be very soothing to a sore throat. Next time you are suffering from a sore throat, add some honey to your tea. You can also make a gargle from honey. Combine two tablespoons of honey with 4 tablespoons of cider vinegar and add a pinch of salt. Gargle this mixture throughout the day to soothe your sore throat.

❑ If you are feeling down from the cold or flu, try mixing this drink containing honey. Take 8 ounces of hot water; add 2 ounces of lemon juice and one tablespoon of honey. If you have eucalyptus oil or ginger root, add it for added benefits. This drink will help your congestion.

❑ Honey is also very healthy for your skin. A mixture of honey and ground almonds will serve as an excellent scrub for your face. For a great moisturizing rinse, mix 2 tablespoons of honey with 2 teaspoons of whole milk. Apply this mix to your face and neck and allow it to settle for 15 minutes. Rinse off 15 minutes later and feel your skin; it will be soft and supple and full of moisture.

❑ If your hair is lacking shine, try honey! Mix one teaspoon of honey with four cups of hot water. Lather throughout your hair and then rinse! Your hair should be full of shine and feel much more moisturized.

❑ Honey can even be used as a mouth rinse. Its antiseptic properties will clean your mouth all while tasting great! Mix one tablespoon of honey with one cup of warm water and rinse throughout your mouth.

❑ If you are diabetic, honey may be a great choice for a sweetener for you. The high level of fructose in honey is absorbed more slowly by your digestive tract than glucose. There is generally not the same sugar rush into your blood stream from honey as there is in standard table sugar. Consult your doctor first on this one, but honey may be a great option for sweetening your food if you are diabetic.

❑ One more use of honey is to control stomach discomfort. Patients with infections, ulcers or inflammation of the gastric system have shown much improvement when they consumed honey. Honey can help fight bacteria that are present in your intestines and also help to heal any ulcers or abscesses. Honey is also proven to help control diarrhoea.

All of these uses of honey are only some of the many benefits honey has on your health. Try to consume a tablespoon of honey daily to benefit your body. The vitamins and minerals contained in honey are a boost to your entire body systems!

What most people don't know is that honey, in addition to tasting good, has an antibacterial activity, due primarily to hydrogen peroxide formed in a slow-release manner by the enzyme glucose oxidase present in honey. Some honeys are no more antibacterial than sugar, while others can be diluted more than 100-fold and still halt the growth of bacteria. The difference in potency of antibacterial activity found among the different honeys is more than 100-fold.

Manuka Honey is the only honey that is tested for its antibacterial activity. It contains an additional antibacterial component found only in honey produced from Leptospermum plants found in New Zealand. Manuka Honey is more effective than other types of honey with hydrogen peroxide against some types of bacteria. For example, Active Manuka Honey is about twice as effective as other honey against the most common causes of infected wounds.

The leader of the world, United States is a little behind in recognizing the amazing potential of Active Manuka Honey as a healing agent. Countries in Europe and other parts of the world have been utilizing Manuka Honey for medicinal purposes for many years. Once it's more recognized in the U.S., Manuka Honey products will be in every medicine cabinet and every doctor's office.

Many medical professionals are now using Active Manuka Honey and are getting good results in patients with wounds that have not responded to standard treatment. It has also been found that Manuka Honey has significant healing properties in healing burns, ulcers, throat and eye infections and is particularly effective with destroying bacteria associated with peptic ulcers. It is also effective as a wound dressing, assisting the healing process.

HONEY AS ANTI BACTERIAL OINTMENT

There are many home remedies that work just as well as any one of the medicines on the pharmacy shelf in the local drug store, but one in particular stands out among the rest. This substance is honey. As everyone knows, honey is made by bees, but it's the process of manufacture that makes it so special, and the ancient Egyptians quickly learned of its amazing abilities.

When bees collect nectar, they carry it back to the hive and regurgitate it into the cells of the honeycomb. Then, with they beat their wings and air dry the water content from the nectar. Enzymes in their saliva change the nectar's sucrose into fructose and glucose, which then binds the remaining water, leaving a percentage between 17 or 18 percent. This process creates an inhospitable substrate where bacteria can't survive. This mixture also is composed of hydrogen peroxide that's made from the enzyme glucose oxidase. Hydrogen peroxide kills bacteria such as e.coli, the ulcer causing bacteria, heliobacter pylori and even staphyloccus. Not many antiseptics can make that same claim.

With all of these amazing traits, honey is an excellent wound treatment. The ancient Egyptians knew this and applied it directly to cuts and scrapes. They also took it orally to maintain internal health and prevent stomach upset. In addition to killing bacteria and preventing bacterial growth, honey is able to aid the body in healing by helping to digest dead tissue and stimulating cells to re-grow new tissue. Honey has been tested on burns, open wounds and stomach ulcers, all with very successful results. With the somewhat recent news of the bacteria killing ability of honey, many people are starting to use it as a homeopathic remedy. However, honey should not be given orally to young children under the age of one, due to the possibility of passing along the dangerous organism chlostridium botulinum, or the bug that causes botulism.

In ancient Egypt, there are many references to the application of honey for wound care and many of the tombs discovered have had jars of crystallized honey carefully placed for use in the after life. Scientists have done research on the quality of honey and have discovered that even thousands of years later, honey, even in its crystallized form, is still an effective anti-bacterial ointment.

The healing ability of honey can vary, depending on which flowers the nectar is from, but all honey kills bacteria. Several papyrus scrolls have been translated that specifically mention honey's healing ability. The Berlin Papyrus from somewhere around 1300 BC, documents the Egyptian's medical knowledge, as well as their mathematical knowledge and the Ebers Papyrus, written about 1500 BC, also mentions using honey and grease to heal wounds.

In ancient Egypt, just as today, the ancient Egyptians received their medical training from more senior physicians and were treated with respect. They were trained in a temple setting, since not only were medicines used, but magical spells as well. It took many years for novice physicians to learn the many treatments and spells for healing, and although they didn't have many of the luxuries and modern medical equipment we do today, they were able to effectively treat and heal the ill by using what nature provided. Sometimes, the simplest and most natural solution is the best.

HONEY PRESERVATION

Due to its unique composition and the complex processing of nectar by the bees which changes its chemical properties, honey is suitable for long term preservation and is easily assimilated even after long conservation. History knows examples of honey preservation for decades, and even centuries. "...small residues of edible honey have even been found in the pharaoh's tombs..."

A number of special prerequisites is, however, necessary to achieve the conservation periods of this order. These might include sealing the product in vessels of chosen material, kept in a favourable environment of specific humidity, temperature etc. An example of natural sealing of the honey with wax by the bees in little separated honey comb cells could be taken for reference.

When conventional preservation methods are applied, it is not recommended to preserve the honey for longer than 2, maximum 3 years. As the honey has a strong tendency to absorb outside smells, it is advisable to keep it in clean, hermetically sealed vessels. It is also advisable to keep it in darkened (not lucid) vessels, or in dark store-places.

When the honey remains in direct sunlight for about one day its lysozyme (antibacterial albuminous enzyme) is being destroyed. Honey should also be protected from oxygen inflow—the accelerated crystallization is brought about by it. Optimal preservation temperature is 4 to 10°C. The store-place should be dark and dry, preventing the honey from absorbing the moisture. When excessive moisture is soaked up by the honey, it might start fermenting. Bee honey can absorb the moisture from the air, therefore it might ferment in a damp place.

Exposure to fresh air brings about the soaking up of external smells, oxygen and moisture, which cause fundamental chemical change of the product—decay of valuable amino acids, vitamins, enzymes and antibiotics. The light has a similar influence.

Due to the above reasons (high tendency to absorb outside smells and moisture) it is not advisable to preserve the honey in a fridge, especially together with other foods and products.

Honey is considered to gradually become toxic when preserved in metal containers. Honey must not be preserved in metal containers, because the acids contained in its structure may cause oxidation. This leads to increased content of heavy metals in honey and decreases the amount of valuable healthy ingredients. Such a honey may cause obnoxious sensations in the stomach.

It used to be preserved in ceramic and wooden containers in ancient times. Glass bottles are recommended nowadays. The wooden vessels of coniferous wood are not suitable for honey preservation. In the oak wood vessels honey grows black.

Traditionally honey was preserved in deep cellars, but not together with wine or other products. It is considered even more sensitive to the store-place conditions than the best wines.

Honey should not be heated above 40°C (104°F).

The best honey is in the uncut honey combs. After being pumped out from there it is very vulnerable, and the main losses of quality take place during preservation and distribution. Heating up to 37°C causes loss of nearly 200 components, part of which are antibacterial. Heating up to 40°C destroys the main bee enzyme, thanks to which the nectar becomes honey; heating up to 50°C turns the honey into caramel (the most valuable honey sugars become analogous to synthetic sugar). Generally any larger temperature fluctuation (10°C is ideal for preservation of ripe honey) causes decay.

Storing Honey

Store honey at room temperature—your kitchen shelf is ideal.

Storing honey in the refrigerator accelerates the honey's crystallization. Crystallization is the natural process in which liquid in honey becomes solid.

If your honey crystallizes, simply place the honey jar in warm water and stir until the crystals dissolve. Or, place the honey in a microwave-safe container with the lid off stirring every 30 seconds, until the crystals dissolve. Be careful not to boil or scorch the honey.

HONEY PROCESSING

There are may processing technique to procure best quality to honey.

Comb Honey

Honey sold still in the original bees' wax comb. Comb honey was once packaged by installing a wooden framework in special honey supers, but this labour intensive method is being replaced by plastic rings or cartridges. With the new approach, a clear cover is usually fitted onto the cartridge after removal from the hive so customers can see the product.

Organic Honey

Organic honey is quite rare to find because most beekeepers routinely use sulfa compounds and antibiotics to control bee diseases, carbolic acid to remove honey from the hive and calcium cyanide to kill colonies before extracting the honey, not to mention that conventional honeybees gather nectar from plants that have been sprayed with pesticides.

Raw Honey

Honey as it exists in the beehive or as obtained by extraction, settling or straining without adding heat above 120 degrees fahrenheit. Raw honey contains some pollen and may contain small particles of wax. Local raw honey is sought after by allergy sufferers as the pollen impurities are thought to lessen the sensitivity to hay fever.

Chunk Honey

Honey packed in widemouth containers consisting of one or more pieces of comb honey surrounded by extracted liquid honey.

Strained Honey

Honey which has been passed through a mesh material to remove particulate material (pieces of wax, propolis, other defects) without removing pollen, minerals or valuable enzymes. Preferred by the health food trade—it may have a cloudy appearance due to the included pollen, and it also tends to crystallize more quickly than ultrafiltered honey.

Ultrafiltered Honey

Honey processed by very fine filtration under high pressure to remove all extraneous solids and pollen grains. The process typically heats honey to 150-170 degrees to more easily pass through the fine filter. Ultrafiltered honey is very clear and has a longer shelf life, because it crystallizes more slowly due to the high temperatures breaking down any sugar seed crystals, making it preferred by the supermarket trade. Ultrafiltration eliminates nutritionally valuable enzymes, such as diastase and invertase.

Heat-Treated Honey

Heat-treatment after extraction reduces the moisture level and destroys yeast cells. Heating liquefies crystals in the honey, too. Heat-exposure does also result in product deterioration, as it increases the level of hydroxymethylfurfural (HMF) and reduces enzyme (*e.g.* diastase) activity. The heat does also affect sensory qualities and reduces the freshness. Heat processing can darken the natural honey colour (browning), too.

Ultrasonicated Honey

Ultrasonication is a non-thermal processing alternative for honey. When honey is exposed to ultrasonication, most of the yeast cells are destroyed. Yeast cells that survive sonication generally lose their ability to grow. This reduces the rate of honey fermentation substantially. Ultrasonication does also eliminate existing crystals and inhibit further crystallization in honey. Ultrasonically aided liquefaction can work at substantially lower temperatures of approx. 35 °C and can reduce liquefaction time to less than 30 seconds.

MEDICINAL USES AND HEALTH EFFECTS

For at least 2700 years, honey has been used to treat a variety of ailments through topical application, but only recently have the antiseptic and antibacterial properties of honey been chemically explained. Wound Gels that contain antibacterial honey and have regulatory approval for wound care are now available to help conventional medicine in the battle against drug resistant strains of bacteria MRSA. As an antimicrobial agent honey may have the potential for treating a variety of ailments. One New Zealand researcher says a particular type of honey may be useful in treating MRSA. Antibacterial properties of honey are the result of the low water activity causing osmosis, hydrogen peroxide effect, and high acidity.Honey may also be used to alleviate the effects of a sore throat. It is mixed with lemon juice and consumed. The mixture coats the throat alleviating discomfort, and the antibacterial, antiseptic properties are good for the throat as well.

In diabetic ulcers

Topical honey has been used successfully in a comprehensive treatment of diabetic ulcers when the patient cannot use other topical antibiotics.

Other medical applications

Some studies suggest that the topical use of honey may reduce odors, swelling, and scarring when used to treat wounds; it may also prevent the dressing from sticking to the healing wound.

Honey has also been used as a treatment for sore throats and coughs for centuries and according to recent research may in fact be more effective than most common medicines.

Honey has been shown to be an effective treatment for conjunctivitis in rats.

Honey (especially when combined with lemon) is often taken orally by pharyngitis and laryngitis sufferers, in order to soothe them.

Though widely believed to alleviate allergies, local honey has been shown to be no more effective than placebos in controlled studies.This may be because most seasonal allergies are caused by tree and grass pollens, which honeybees do not collect.

❏❏

PRECAUTIONS AND HEALTH BENEFITS

Due to the natural presence of botulinum endospores in honey, children under one year of age should not be given honey. The more developed digestive systems of older children and adults generally destroy the spores. Infants, however, can contract botulism from honey.

Honey produced from the flowers of rhododendrons, mountain laurels, sheep laurel and azaleas may cause honey intoxication. Symptoms include dizziness, weakness, excessive perspiration, nausea and vomiting. Less commonly, low blood pressure, shock, heart rhythm irregularities and convulsions may occur, with rare cases resulting in death. Honey intoxication is more likely when using 'natural' unprocessed honey and honey from farmers who may have a small number of hives. Commercial processing, with pooling of honey from numerous sources generally dilutes any toxins.

Some more Precautions

Do not add honey to your baby's food, water or formula.
Do not dip your baby's pacifier in honey.
Do not give your baby honey as medicine.

Honey may contain Clostridium botulinum spores that can cause infant botulism—a rare but serious disease that affects the nervous system of young babies (under one year of age). C. botulinum spores are present throughout the environment and may be found in dust, soil and improperly canned foods. Adults and children over one year of age are routinely exposed to, but not normally affected by, C. botulinum spores.

Health Benefits of Honey

Research has shown that unlike most other sweeteners, honey contains small amounts of a wide array of vitamins, minerals, amino acids and antioxidants.

Honey, a rich source of carbohydrates, provides a quick source of energy.

Honey's unique composition makes it an effective antimicrobial agent, useful for treating minor burns and scrapes, and for aiding the treatment of sore throats and other bacterial infections.

Why do Bees make Honey?

We know that bees have been producing honey as they do today for at least 150 million years. Bees produce honey as food stores for the hive during the long months of winter when flowers aren't blooming and therefore little or no nectar is available to them. European honey bees, genus Apis Mellifera, produce such an abundance of honey, far more than the hive can eat, that humans can harvest the excess. For this reason, European honey bees can be found in beekeeper's hives around the world!

RAW HONEY

Raw honey is the concentrated nectar of flowers that comes straight from the extractor; it is the only unheated, pure, unpasteurized, unprocessed honey. An alkaline-forming food, this type of honey contains ingredients similar to those found in fruits, which become alkaline in the digestive system. It doesn't ferment in the stomach and it can be used to counteract acid indigestion. When mixed with ginger and lemon juices, it also relieves nausea and supplies energy. Raw honey is the healthiest choice amongst the various forms of honey as it has the most nutritional value and contains amylase, an enzyme concentrated in flower pollen which helps predigest starchy foods like breads.

Most honeys found in the market are not raw honey but 'commercial' honey, which has been heated and filtered so that it looks cleaner and smoother, more appealing on the shelf, and easier to handle and package. When honey is heated, its delicate aromas, yeast and enzymes which are responsible for activating vitamins and minerals in the body system are partially destroyed.

Hence, such honey is not as nutritious as raw honey.

Characterised by fine textured crystals, raw honey looks milkier and contains particles and flecks made of bee pollen, honeycomb bits, propolis, and broken bee wing fragments. Raw and unfiltered honey is relatively low in moisture content (14% to 18%) and has a high antioxidant level. It will usually granulate and crystallize to a margarine-like consistency after a month or two. Many people prefer to spread it on bread and waffles, dissolve it in hot coffee or tea, or use it for cooking and baking.

Among manufacturers there exists no uniform code of using the term 'raw honey'. There are no strict legal requirements for claiming and labelling honey as 'raw'. You may find raw honey that are unprocessed but slightly warmed to retard granulation for a short period of time and allow light straining and packing into containers for sale. In this case, the honey will not be considered 100% 'raw' because it has been heated slightly and therefore rightfully should not be labeled as such by the supplier. Using as little heat as possible is a sign of careful handling.

Honey comes in a number of physical forms, and understanding the variety will certainly help you pick a more appropriate form from the market when you wish to combine honey with other ingredients used in the preparation of foods. Try out the various forms and tastes of honey when you have the chance!

1. Comb Honey : It is difficult to find comb honey nowadays, but sometimes you can find a jar of liquid honey to which a piece of cut comb has been added. Before the invention of honey extracting device, honey is mostly produced in the form of comb honey. Today, very little honey is produced as comb honey.

Comb honey is raw pure honey sections taken straight

from the hive—honey bees' wax comb with no further handling at all. It is the most unprocessed form in which honey comes—the bees fill the hexagon shaped wax cells of the comb with honey and cap it with beeswax. You can eat comb honey just like a chewy candy. Because the honey in the comb is untouched and is deemed to be pure, honey presented in this form comes with a a relatively higher price tag.

Liquid honey has been filtered to remove fine particles, pollen grains, and air bubbles, and heated to melt visible crystals after being extracted from the honey comb by centrifugal force or gravity. Because liquid honey mixes easily into a variety of foods, its uses are diverse. It is used as a syrup for pancakes and waffles and in a wide variety of recipes, and it's especially convenient for cooking and baking.

Cream honey : If you are one of those who complain that honey is messy to use, cream honey, which is also known as whipped honey, spun honey, granulated honey, or honey fondant, would be an excellent alternative to liquid honey. As the crystallisation process has been controlled very precisely, cream honey does not drip like liquid honey, has a smooth consistency and can be spread like butter.

It has one part finely granulated honey blended with nine parts liquid honey. Crystallisation lightens the colour of honey, but does not affect the taste and nutritional goodness at all. For instance, creamed premium lavender honey from the south of France is white in the jar. For those who live in warm climate countries like India, probably might have noticed that the creamed honey that you buy from the air-conditioned food chain store becomes darker in colour and more runny when placed in room temperature.

Caution : Honey does not remain stable if the moisture

content is too high. No reputable honey supplier would add water to honey, as this would cause the honey to ferment and emit an alcoholic smell.

Colour and Flavour of Honey

Colour is used in the honey industry as a convenient measure of honey flavour and aroma. Generally, lighter honeys have a milder flavour and darker honeys have a more robust flavour. The colour and flavour of honey is largely determined by the floral source of the nectar. However, exposure to heat and storage time may affect honey's quality and colour. Normally, the darkening of honey occurs more rapidly when honey is stored at high temperatures. Also, honey appears lighter in colour after it has granulated, which is why most creamed honeys are opaque and light in colour.

❒❒

HONEY FOR BEAUTY

Our skin has a natural protective barrier of fats that creates a nice smooth waterproof layer to keep the moisture in and foreign substances out. The skin's ability to stay hydrated is an important factor in its ability to maintain softness, suppleness and elasticity. Unfortunately, the drying effect of the cold weather, the damaging effect of the harsh sun and pollution from the environment can cause our skin to look fatigue, dull and blotchy.

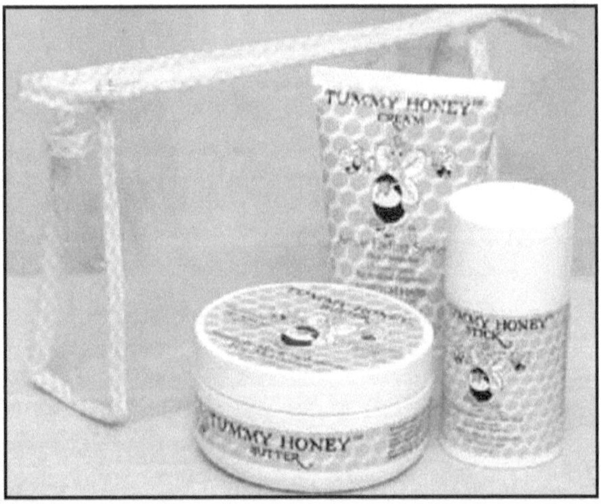

Anti Aging

Honey is a great natural anti aging skin care product. Throughout the centuries, legendary beauties like Cleopatra and Poppea, wife of Roman Emperor Nero have used raw honey as part of their skin and hair care treatments to keep them looking youthful. This natural healing agent contains an enzyme called glucose oxidase, that when combined with water, produces hydrogen peroxide, a mild antiseptic. In addition to the glucose oxidase enzyme, honey also contains antioxidants and flavonoids that may function as antibacterial agents. Honey is also a natural moisturizer. It is a humectant, having the ability attract and retain moisture, and to rebuild the moisture level in the skin without making it oily. It helps replenish necessary skin moisture, especially during the winter months. This is why honey is a popular anti aging skin care ingredient in many commercial moisturizing products including cleansers, creams, shampoos, shower gels, and conditioners. And because it's so gentle, it is suitable for sensitive skin and baby care products.

Weight Loss

Honey and weight loss are often associated.

Refined dietary sugars lack minerals and vitamins and are often called empty calories. They draw upon the body's nutrients to be metabolized into the system, and when these nutrients are depleted, metabolizing of cholesterol and fatty acid is impeded, contributing to higher cholesterol and promoting obesity due to higher fatty acid on the organs and tissues. The good news is that honey, a natural sweetener, on the other hand, contains 22 amino acids and a variety of minerals essential for its metabolism and hence is helpful in preventing obesity. It is believed that drinking lemon juice with a little honey the first thing in the morning is an effective anti cellulite treatment as it helps to increase body metabolism. If you are determined to shed weight and speed up your sluggish metabolism, try this honey and lemon diet tip. If you like, another very popular recipe associated with honey and weight loss is a drink that uses honey and cinnamon as ingredients. Many people have found this home remedy very effective in losing weight. The steps are easy: Dissolve half a teaspoon of cinnamon powder (or ground cinnamon) in a cup of boiling water. Stir the mixture and cover for half an hour. Filter away any big particles and add a teaspoon of honey. Take it in the morning with an empty stomach about half an hour before breakfast.

For people who tend to overeat or feel discomfort in the stomach after meals, honey can be taken for better digestion. Honey is a simple carbohydrate that one safely take during fasting because it contains easily digested sugars. Foods that are rich in sugars or complexes of sugars are carbohydrates. How the sugars are arranged will determine whether we call a food a source of simple or complex carbohydrates. When sugars are bound into rows, as they are in starches such as whole grains and legumes, they are called complex carbohydrates. It takes the body much longer to digest the sugar from a complex carbohydrate.

The latest theory based on the hibernation diet also builds a link between fructose-rich honey and weight loss. It suggests taking a generous spoonful or two of honey at night, either as a warm drink or straight from the jar, and promises to help us sleep and lose weight at the same time by fuelling the liver, speeding up fat-burning metabolism and easing stress hormones.

❐❐

HONEY AND SKIN CARE

There may be no better way to bring a smooth glow to your skin than by using skin care products containing honey. Honey's ability to absorb and retain moisture make it an ideal ingredient in many cosmetics as it helps keep skin hydrated and fresh. In fact, history shows that ancient beauties regularly applied a mixture of honey and milk to the face to keep their skin looking young, radiant and smooth.

Honey's natural antioxidant and antimicrobial properties help to protect the skin from the damage of the sun's rays while supporting the skin's ability to rejuvenate and refresh depleted skin. One advantage of using honey as a natural skin care ingredient is for the treatment of acne. Honey absorbs impurities from the pores in the skin, making it an ideal cleansing agent. There is also an increasing number of honey products being introduced to the market for hair care, skin care, hand lotions, facial masks, moisturizers, wound care, etc.

Really, there is no simpler way to bring a smooth glow to your skin than with honey beauty recipes. Honey's ability to absorb and retain moisture make it an ideal ingredient in a lot of cosmetics as it helps keep skin hydrated and fresh and prevents drying. It is known that ancient beauties regularly applied a mixture of honey and milk to the face to keep the skin young-looking, radiant, and smooth.

Honey's natural antioxidant and anti-microbial properties help to protect the skin from the damage of the sun's rays, supports the skin's ability to rejuvenate and refresh depleted skin, leaving it feeling silky soft and supple. One of the most common skin benefits of honey is related to minor acne treatment. Honey absorbs impurities from the pores on the skin, making it an ideal cleansing agent. With the wide-ranging of honey and skin care recipes, it is no wonder that there exists a huge number of honey products in the market for hair care, baby care, skin care for sunscreen, hand lotions, facial scrubs and moisturizers. And for instance, the Manuka Honey Lip Balm is an effective and natural moisturizer. It contains sun protection properties to soothe and protect the lips from becoming dry and chapped in cold and dry weather.

Here are some do-it-yourself, self-help, extremely easy to follow recipes to enjoy the benefits of honey in skin care. All the ingredients that go along with them are so easily accessible.

Cucumber-Honey Toner *:* Puree 1 cucumber in a blender and drain away the liquid. Add 2 teaspoons of honey and mix. Apply on the face and neck area with a cotton pad. Air dry it and rinse clean.

Honey-Apple Toner : In a blender or food processor,

combine 1 peeled, cored apple with a tablespoon of honey and pulse until smooth. Apply mixture to face and allow it to stay for 15 minutes, then rinse.

Honey-Oats Face Scrub : Combine 1 tablespoon honey, 1 tablespoon finely-ground almonds, 2 tablespoons dry oatmeal, and some lemon juice or yogurt to a luxurious and exfoliating facial scrub. Massage mixture gently onto face, then rinse with warm water.

Gentle Honey Cleanser : Mix 1/4 cup honey, 1 tablespoon liquid soap and 1/2 cup glycerin (found in drug stores). Apply gently on to face using a face sponge. Rinse with warm water and pat face dry.

Hot Honey Bath : Perhaps the easiest beauty recipe related to honey and skin care—Add 1/4 cup of honey to your hot bath water for silky and luscious skin.

Honey Hair Conditioning Treatment : For lustrous, silky, healthy hair and scalp, simply combine 1/2 cup honey and 2 tablespoons to 1/4 cup olive oil. Massage scalp with this conditioner, then put on a shower cap for 30 minutes. Shampoo and rinse as usual.

Honey Facial

A honey facial is wonderful especially if you haven't experience one before. Honey facial cleansing mask is safe for your skin. Around the world facials containing Manuka honey are gaining acceptance as the norm for a facial. Regardless of your age or your skin condition, using a good manuka honey facial cleanse will help your skin look younger. The issue has been and will always be what type of honey is being used in the facial cleanser or mask. Honey has long been understood for its antiseptic and healing qualities, but different honeys from different parts of the world have different levels of active ingredients. This means some honeys are better than others for skin care. Honeys from North America tend towards being clover based, as the bees that make the honey gather their nectar from clover. Bees in New Zealand gather their nectar from the Tea Tree, a plant that is unique to New Zealand. The bees there produce a honey called Manuka honey and of that there are two versions Active Manuka Honey and Manuka Honey. Hence, manuka honey facial products such as the cleansing mask is perfect for skin with problems.

Even sensitive skins can benefit from this specialized honey facial. Active Manuka Honey has absolutely amazing properties for rejuvenation of human skin. It kills bacteria, maintains moisture, removes free radicals, soothes wounds and reduces inflammation. All of these claims have been proven. The ingredients of a high quality Manuka honey face gel work in concert with your own skin and immune system to produce great results. What then makes this face gel so very special? The reality is most people simply won't take any time to research products and understand what ingredients work and what ingredients are actually bad for your skin. Manuka honey extracts are very well tolerated on the skin and can be used safely for children. One of the best skin care honey products is Deep active cleansing mask. Due to its unique properties, this cleansing mask is much sought after by people who are aware of what it can do.

HONEY V/s SUGAR

Honey v/s Sugar. What are their differences?

Both sweeteners contain glucose and fructose. However, for sugar, in the process of manufacturing, the organic acids, protein, nitrogen elements, enzymes and vitamins in the sugar cane are destroyed, whereas honey, a natural sweetener, subjects only to minimal heating. Also, honey has certain beneficial antioxidant and antimicrobial properties which are not present in table sugar.

Here are three honey nutrition facts that will make you feel good about eating honey:

One tablespoon of table sugar or sucrose contains 46 calories, while one tablespoon of natural sweetener honey has 64 calories. Though honey may have more calories, we actually need to use less of it since it is sweeter than table sugar. As a result, you may in fact consume even less amount of calories that you would with sugar. And in the long run even though honey is more expensive, it may be more economical than table sugar.

Table sugar is sucrose, which is made up of two molecules bonded together. When we eat table sugar, our stomach has to use its own enzymes to separate the molecules apart before we can use the sugar's energy. Honey is quite different. The bees have added a special enzyme to the nectar that divides the sucrose into glucose and fructose—two simple sugars for our bodies can absorb directly.

Hence, compared to table sugar, honey has a healthier Glycemic Index (GI) which measures the negative impact of a given food on the blood-glucose level. The lower the GI rating, the slower the absorption and infusion of sugars into the bloodstream and hence a more gradual and healthier digestion process.

Unlike honey, table sugar lacks minerals and vitamins (hence it's been often called empty calories), they draw upon the body's nutrients to be metabolized into the system. When these nutrients are all used up, metabolizing of undesirable cholesterol and fatty acid is impeded, contributing to higher cholesterol and promoting obesity due to higher fatty acid on the organs and tissues. That is why it is not uncommon for fat people to suffer from malnutrition and many other health related problems. So the message is, honey v/s sugar, if you are watching your weight, honey will be a smarter choice than sugar. Besides the differences in nutrition, sugar can never compete with honey in taste. Though both are sweet, honey has such a unique flavour that can be very useful and superior in many foods and beverages. The range of honey floral varieties is so vast that experiencing for yourself the uniqueness of each variety and being able to appropriate each variety to exploit every possibility to complement and improve taste of different types of foods becomes a skillful art.

❐❐

COOKING TIPS WITH HONEY

Cooking with honey gives you a never-ending list of possibilities and recipes due to the many practical functions honey could serve.

Enhances browning and crisp : great for glazing roasted and baked foods to promote surface browning.

Is a flavour enhancer : an always welcomed natural sweetener for hot teas and cold beverages, especially when there is a huge variety of flavours of honey.

Provides texture and feel : an excellent addition in pastries and cakes making.

Prolongs shelf-life : a natural preservative for pickles and sauces.

Retains moisture : an essential ingredient for providing the moisture in rich cakes and prolonging the moisture retention.

Is binding due to its viscosity : a brilliant ingredient that aids shaping of desserts such as pastries, puddings, and cakes.

Adds colour : contributes a delightful golden hue to sauces, dressings, jellies, and frozen desserts.

6 Useful Tips

1. As a general guide, when using honey recipes, use less of honey because it is almost twice as sweet as sugar. Replace one cup of sugar for half a cup of honey, and because honey is hygroscopic (meaning it attracts water), reduce the amount of liquid in the recipe by 1/4 cup for each cup of honey added.

2. Give longer time for beating and more vigorous beating compared to sugar recipes, and when baking with honey.

3. Add 1/2 teaspoon baking soda for each cup of honey used. This will neutralize honey's acidity and help the food rise.

4. Reduce the oven temperature by 25 degrees Fahrenheit. Honey batter becomes crisp and browns faster than sugar batter.

5. When using honey in jams, jellies, or candies, increase the cooking temperature juqst a bit to allow the extra liquid to evaporate.

6. The floral variety of the honey should be considered when cooking with honey since honey has the power to balance, enhance or impart some of its flavour to other foods. The fascinating number of honey varieties and their versatility in cooking is the reason to the thousands of tantalizing recipes using honey out there.

❑❑❑

www.ingramcontent.com/pod-product-compliance
Lightning Source LLC
LaVergne TN
LVHW100406181026
850499LV00037B/626
* 9 7 8 8 1 3 1 0 0 7 4 3 3 *